THIS BOOK BELONGS TO

Color Test

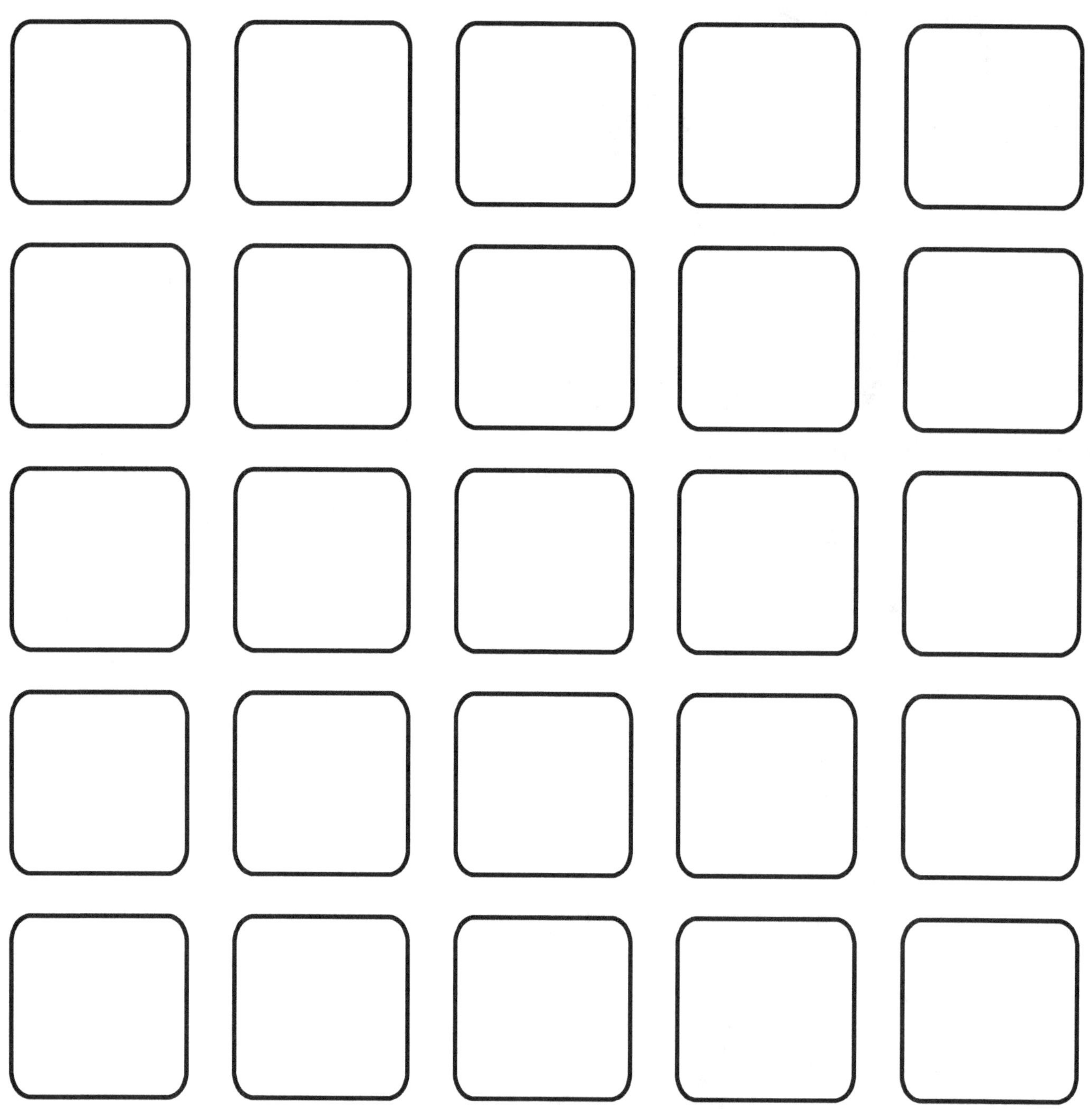

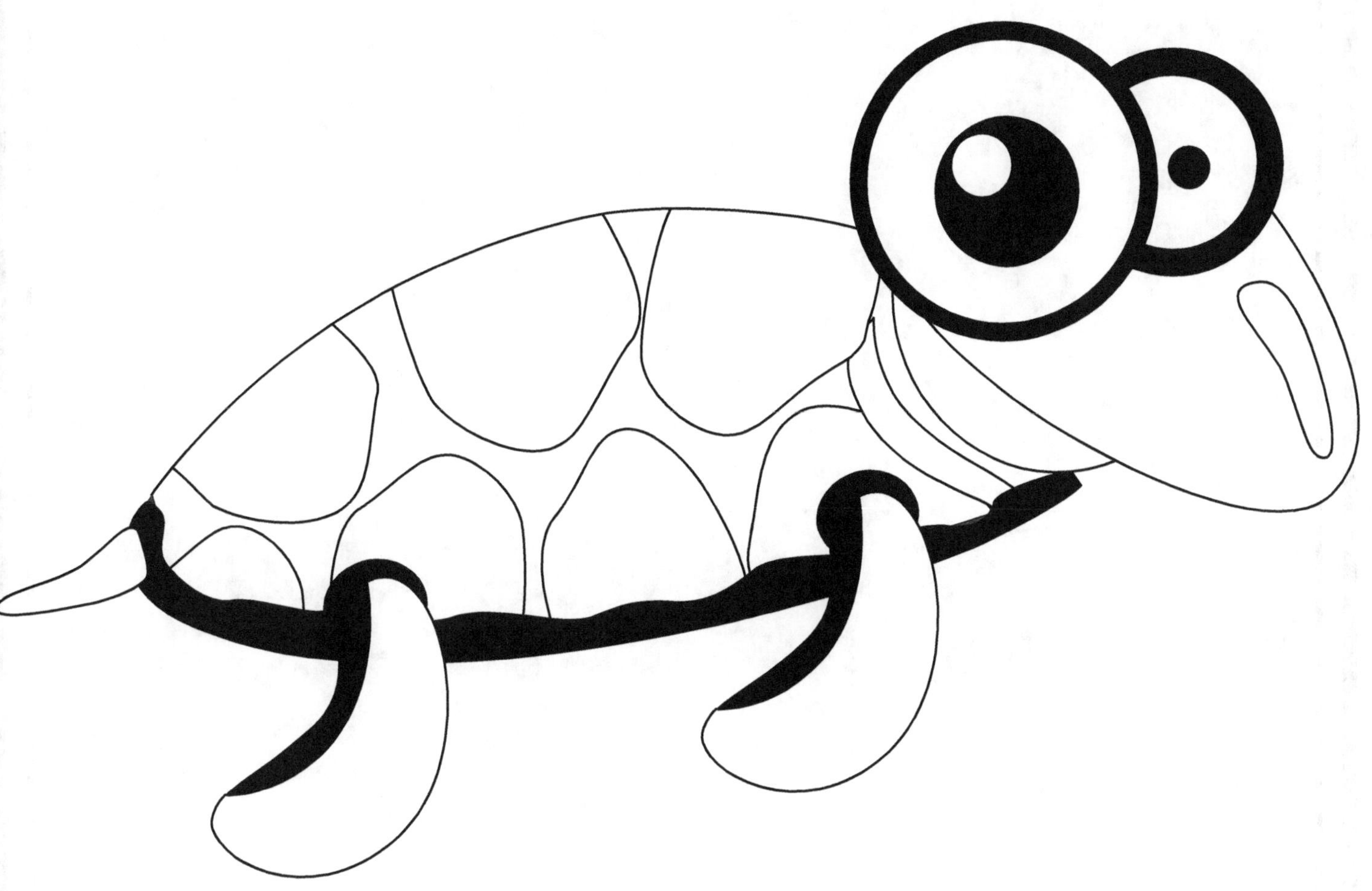

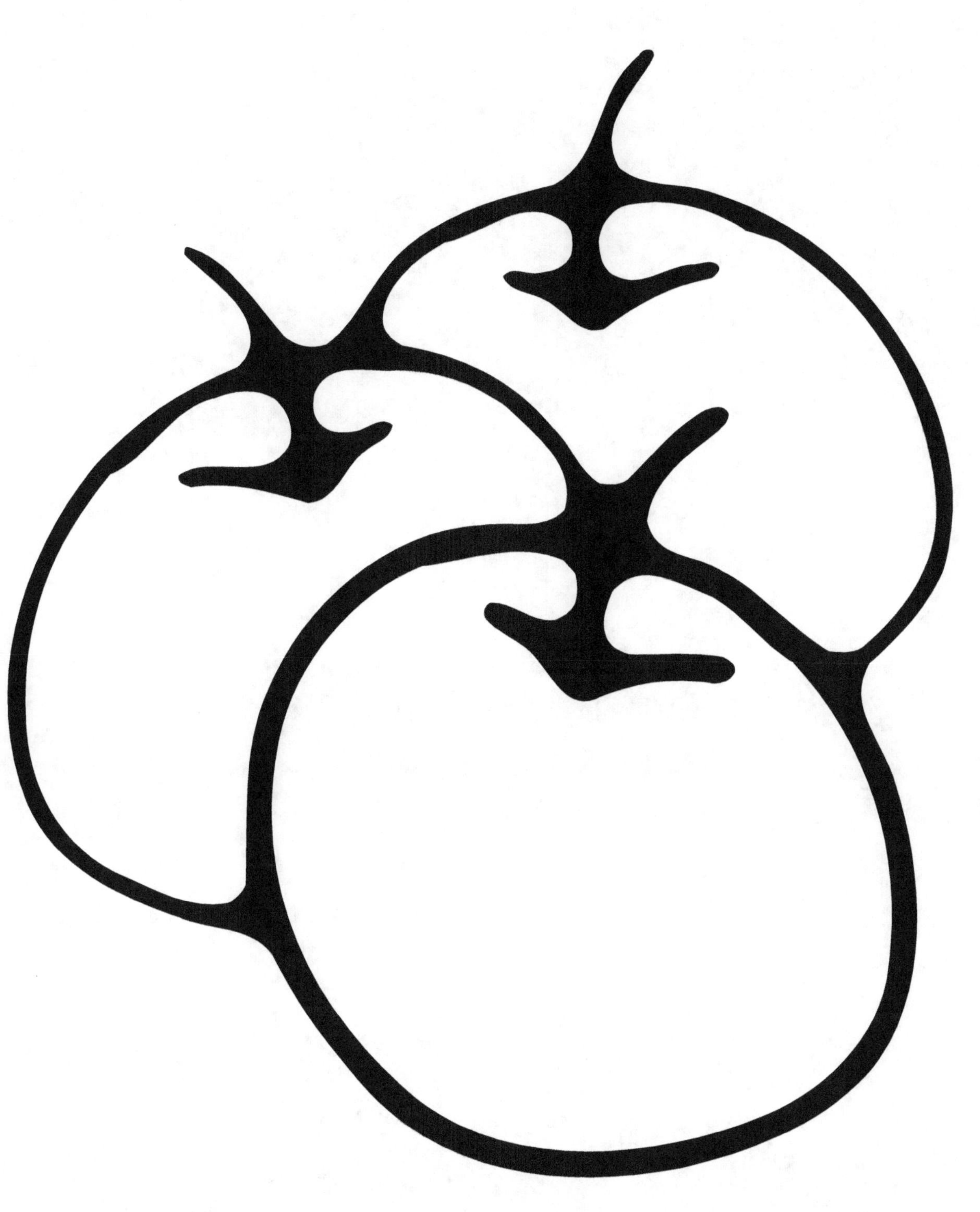

12

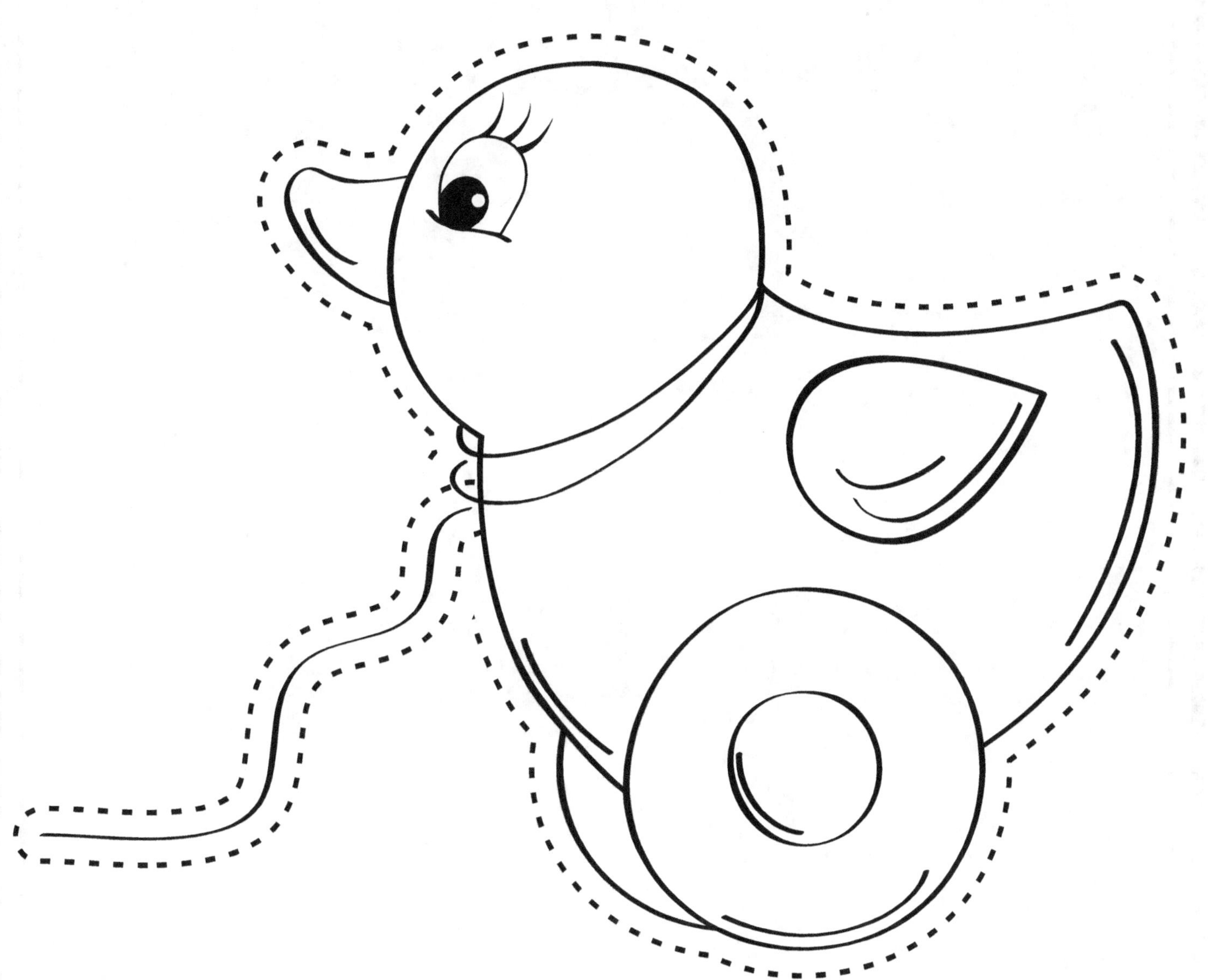

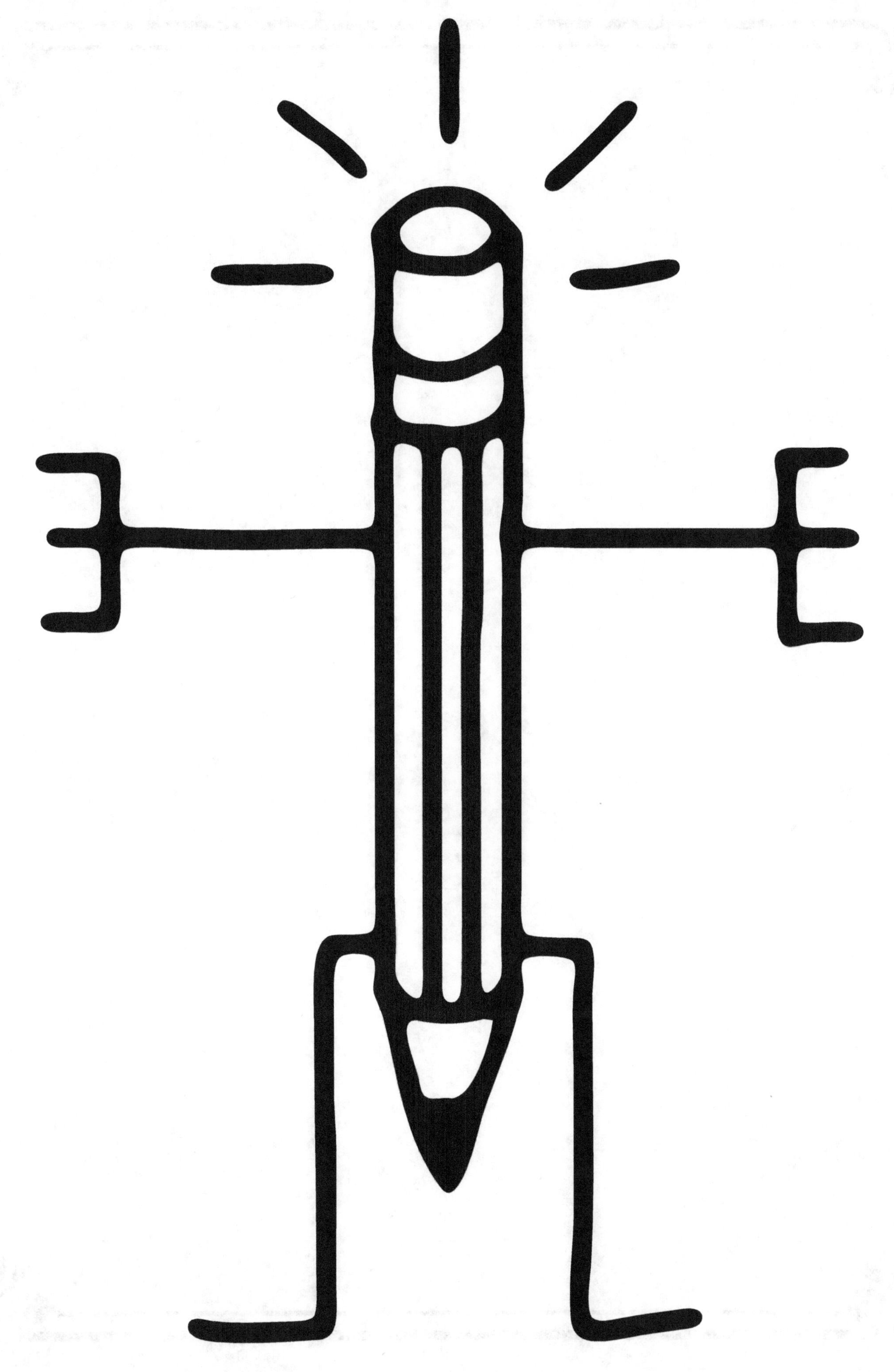

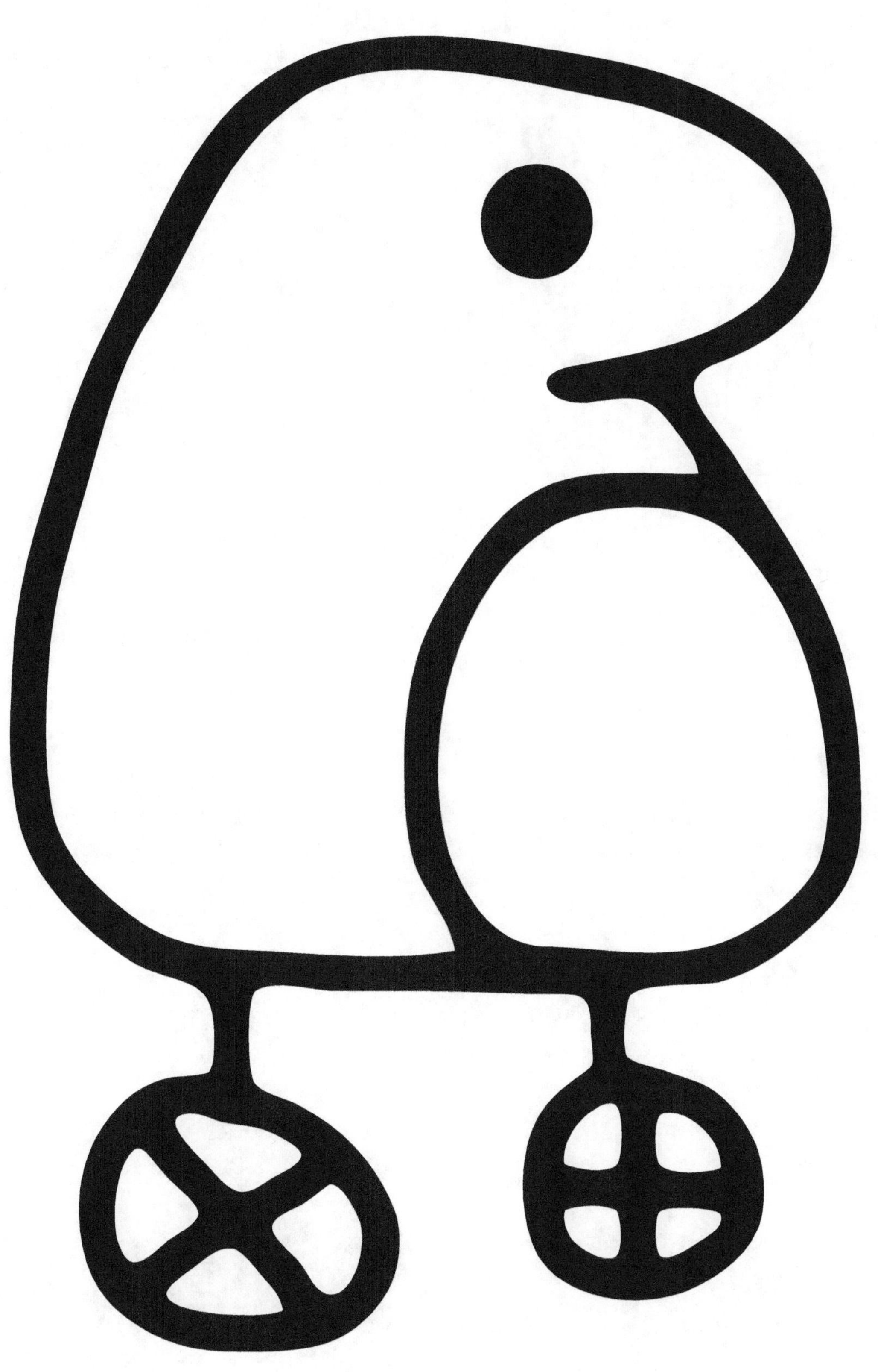